THE HOBBIT™

AN UNEXPECTED JOURNEY

The World of Hobbits

First U.S. edition

Text by Paddy Kempshall
First published by HarperCollins *Children's Books* in 2012

The Hobbit: An Unexpected Journey: The World of Hobbits is a companion to the film *The Hobbit: An Unexpected Journey*
and is published with the permission, but not the approval, of the Estate of the late J.R.R. Tolkien.
Dialogue quotations are from the film, not the novel.

The Hobbit is published in the United States by Houghton Mifflin Harcourt.

www.hmhbooks.com

Library of Congress Cataloging-in-Publication Data is available.
ISBN 978-0-547-89873-5

Printed in the United States
HC 10 9 8 7 6 5 4 3 2 1

THE HOBBIT™

AN UNEXPECTED JOURNEY

The World of Hobbits

MIDDLE -EARTH

Houghton Mifflin Harcourt
Boston   New York
2012

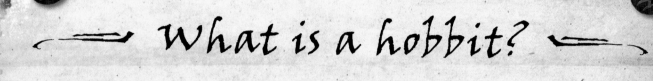

What is a hobbit?

There never was quite such an unexpected (or unwilling) hero as a hobbit, but in the history of Middle-earth it was this group of small people that had some of the biggest adventures.

But what is a hobbit? These days they are rare creatures and very shy of us Big People. But never fear, because in these pages you can learn all there is to know about a wondrous folk who are full of good cheer, good times and good food!

From their homes to their friends, enemies, adventures and favourite foods (of which there are quite a few...) there is much more to these little people than meets the eye. So if you would like to find out more, then read on and enter the world of hobbits...

Bilbo Baggins

FROM HEAD TO TOE

There's certainly more to a hobbit than a friendly face and round belly. A curious race, hobbits are not as adventurous as Men (or the Big People as they like to call them), nor are they as broad and strong as Dwarves, but they have hidden strengths and skills all of their own.

You wouldn't mistake a hobbit for a Dwarf, nor would you think one was an Elf or even a fully-grown Man. Instead, hobbits have their own individual look and style.

Living in their own quiet little world, far from the cares and troubles of the rest of Middle-earth, hobbits lead a life that some might consider unadventurous and boring, but many would think perfect.

Hobbits are often called halflings by those who don't know any better. This gives you a clue to one of the first things you will notice about a hobbit if you are ever lucky enough to meet one – they really aren't very tall!

Smaller even than Dwarves, most hobbits measure a rather short and solid 3 feet in height. Some hobbits have been known to reach the extraordinary heights of 4 feet, but over the years it seems that the average height of a hobbit may even have shrunk! In fact it is not uncommon to find some hobbits who are as short as 2 feet!

Hobbits live for a very long time – far longer than Men. Indeed most hobbits are thought to be in middle-age at 70, and many have been known to reach their 100th birthday! One of the oldest hobbits who ever lived was even older than that – a certain Bilbo Baggins.

Of course, living for such a long time can have its problems, especially if your parents live for a long time too. In the world of hobbits you aren't seen by your parents as being a grown-up until you are at least 33 years old!

Friendly faces

While Dwarves believe a great beard is something to be proud of (even if you're female!), most hobbits are unable to grow them – though they don't seem to have the same problem growing their bellies!

Under their thick, curly hair you would notice something else quite odd about hobbits – their pointed ears. Though not as pointed as the ears of an Elf, a hobbit's ears are very good at listening and hearing the slightest sound. Especially if that sound happens to be someone calling them for dinner!

A hobbit's clothes

Most hobbits dress in quite bright colours, with yellows and greens being particular favourites. Their clothes are sensible, smart and above all, practical. You're more likely to catch a hobbit wearing an apron for cooking than armour for fighting, that's for sure.

Feet first

Being extremely sensible people, it's a bit of a surprise to find that, no matter the weather, or where they are, hobbits don't wear shoes. However, it's really only a surprise until you notice a hobbit's feet – and it's quite hard to miss them! Hobbits have very large feet – much larger than someone so short should have – and they are covered in thick curly hair.

The skin on their feet is extremely tough, especially on the bottom. That means hobbits can walk anywhere, wandering about over any sort of ground, without needing any shoes or socks!

Even though their feet are large, hobbits are still able to move very quickly and skilfully. Many of them can walk around without making any noise at all, even in the thickest forest or on the stoniest ground.

Adventure and excitement

Hobbits are usually very down-to-earth, and the most excitement they like in their life is when they find another cake in the pantry. To most hobbits, adventures aren't good things. As Bilbo says, they are "Nasty disturbing uncomfortable things. Make you late for dinner!" Any hobbit who is keen on having adventures is an odd and unusual hobbit indeed.

It just so happens that in all the history of Middle-earth, some of the greatest heroes who had the most exciting adventures were hobbits. They didn't all just decide to head off on an adventure though, but were convinced to come along by the powerful wizard, Gandalf.

Indeed, Gandalf seems to have quite a knack for finding a certain kind of unusually adventurous hobbit and getting them to rush off and follow him on his epic quests. After a visit from Gandalf, some hobbits have actually been so keen to begin their journey that they leave home without their handkerchief. Which, as any hobbit will tell you, is not very sensible at all.

A HOBBIT'S HOME

Like Elves and Dwarves, hobbits only live in certain parts of the world, and in far fewer places than many of the other peoples that live in Middle-earth. Hobbits aren't fond of large towns, full of cramped streets and tall buildings. Instead they prefer to make their homes in small towns and villages in the countryside.

Most hobbits love their home so much that many of them have never left it or travelled any further into Middle-earth. To most hobbits, wanting to travel and see far-off places is a bit odd. When you learn a little more about where hobbits have made their homes, you might just agree and wonder why anyone would want to go anywhere else.

The land of hobbits

Most hobbits can be found living in a place called the Shire. Far to the west of Middle-earth, the Shire is a peaceful and pleasant land full of gentle hills and green fields. Almost rectangular in shape, it is snuggled between the Hills of Evendim to the North, marshes to the South and the Blue Mountains and Grey Havens to the West. The Brandywine river lies to the east of the Shire and is generally agreed as the edge of the land of the hobbits. Beyond it lies the Misty Mountains and the rest of Middle-earth.

MIDDLE-EARTH

The fields of the Shire aren't just pretty places to take a long walk after luncheon, they are also places full of food! Whether it is an orchard of plump apples, a field full of bee hives and honeycombs or a well-cared-for patch of carrots or beans, you'll find many delicious things growing in the Shire. Good food is a very important part of a hobbit's life, so wherever you go in the Shire you can be sure that you'll not be too far away from a table full of delicious, home-cooked food made with the freshest and best ingredients.

The Shire isn't an empty place and there are some areas that contain lots of hobbits. Rather than all living together in one big city, hobbits tend to prefer living close together in smaller villages.

Hobbits aren't the only ones who love their homeland. Even powerful wizards like Gandalf can't help but come back to the Shire time and again to take a moment to slow down and enjoy its sweet air and simple life.

A very fine place to live

Hobbits don't really live in houses – lots of them live in holes in the ground! Not nasty, dirty, wet little holes full of bugs and strange smells, but hobbit-holes. Hobbit-holes are very comfortable, cosy places and come in lots of different shapes and sizes, a bit like the hobbits who live in them!

If you were at tea and asked a hobbit to tell you about a particularly fine hobbit-hole, most of them would tell you about Bag End. Bag End is dug into the side of the Hill, just north of Hobbiton. It is at the end of Bagshot Row which snakes up the Hill and it is the home of Bilbo Baggins. Bag End has been in Bilbo's family for many years and is the most charming place to live.

Outside the walls of Bag End are pretty flower gardens, as well as a large garden for growing all sorts of tasty vegetables. Hobbits just love to grow things, especially if they can then eat the things they've grown! On top of the Hill is an old oak tree. Inside Bag End, the rooms are clean, but filled with all sorts of clutter from members of the Baggins family who have lived there over the years.

Hobbits like to use circles when they build their houses and Bag End is no different. Its windows are all round and it also has a perfectly round, green front door, with a round brass knob in the middle. If you opened the front door and walked inside, you would see a very fine hall, a bit like a tunnel, that curves back into the hillside.

When Gandalf paid Bilbo a visit, he carved a very special symbol into the door of Bag End without Bilbo knowing. It didn't look like much to most people, but to Thorin and his 12 Dwarf companions it was a clear sign that inside was just the sort of brave person they needed to help them!

Inside Bag End

On the left side of the hall are all the best rooms (also with round doors). They are the best because they are the only rooms to have windows that look out over the fields and gardens below. This means that they are perfect for catching the sunshine to help warm your toes while you have a spot of tea and decide what to have for dinner.

Bag End's floors have either carpets or tiles and the walls are covered in wood, with many pegs for the hats and coats of all the hobbits who come to visit. There are no stairs in a hobbit-hole. Every room is on the same level, from bedrooms, to sitting rooms, and from kitchens to dining rooms and pantries (there are lots of these!). Of course, being the home of a hobbit means that the ceilings aren't very high, so if you do ever go to visit, be sure to mind your head!

As you might expect, the kitchen in Bag End is one of its finest rooms. With a scrubbed table and pantries bursting with delicious treats, it is welcoming and cosy, yet large enough to make sure that even 13 hungry Dwarves feel at home and have somewhere to sit and enjoy their food.

april

Sterday	1	8	15 tuckBorough Market	22	29
Sunday	dinner with amaranth at Brandy hall 2	9	16	23	30
Monday	3	10	17	24	—eggs —flour —seedcakes
Trewsday	smoke ring contest at the ivy Bush 4	11	18	25	get seed potatoes from the gaffer and plant them during the third week
hevensday	5	12	19	26	

Whether it's their clothes, their day or their food, there's nothing a hobbit likes more in life than for things to be plain, simple and predictable. Hobbits love an unexciting life, full of simple pleasures and good friends — so it's easy to see why so many people in Middle-earth enjoy spending time with them!

A quiet life doesn't mean that the world of hobbits is boring. Hobbits most definitely believe that you should take every chance to enjoy life and to get the most out of it. But a hobbit also knows that you can have a very rich and happy life without needing to be part of any adventures.

Watching the world go by

Hobbits prefer doing jobs that help them live a quiet, normal and peaceful life. You won't find many Warg tamers in the Shire, but you're quite likely to run into lots of farmers, gardeners, blacksmiths and cooks. In fact hobbits seem to spend a lot of their time doing jobs that have something to do with food!

If you're looking for excitement, then the hobbit life is not for you. A hobbit would rather sit in the sun on his doorstep and watch the cows munch on grass or chat about the weather than go racing off across Middle-earth in search of fame, riches and adventure.

Friends, family and good company mean much more to hobbits than money – something that makes them quite unusual compared to Dwarves and their love of gems, or Men and their desire for power.

The visits of the great Gandalf the Grey were something of a hot topic in the Shire. While hobbits like Gandalf very much, those of a more practical and respectable nature frown upon his more 'exciting' ways. Gandalf always seems to bring dreadful, unexpected adventures with him or persuade usually sensible hobbits to rush off on some great quest. The fuss and bother that this causes is something that the more sensible hobbits of the Shire could well do without.

Food, glorious food

Anyone who has ever seen a hobbit would be able to tell from their cheerful face and round belly that they enjoy good food and good times. You might even say that to a hobbit, food is the most important thing in the world. Which is quite a sensible attitude when you think about it – after all, you know where you are with a good cup of tea and a slice of cake.

Hobbits love food so much that their whole day seems to be spent doing nothing but eating. In fact, for a hobbit it's a very unusual (and most unwelcome) day if it doesn't have at least six or seven different meals in it.

While hobbits might like to eat a lot, they don't eat many unusual foods. Bread, meat, potatoes and cheese are all delightful choices for a hobbit meal, as well as cakes. Lots of cakes.

Perhaps some of the tastiest treats for a hobbit, however, are mushrooms. Many a young hobbit has spent time mushroom hunting, sometimes even going so far as to 'hunt' them right out of a farmer's field and into their pockets!

Mealtimes for hobbits are times to be shared, especially with good friends. As hobbits don't believe in rushing any of the good things in life, it is usual for a meal in their company to last quite a long time. More often than not these meals will also include lots of singing too.

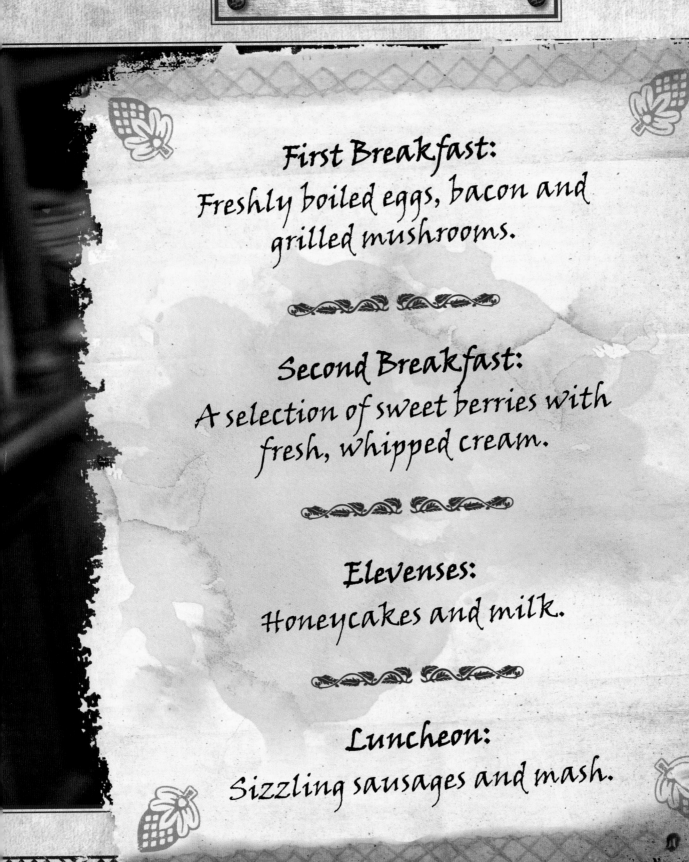

First Breakfast:

Freshly boiled eggs, bacon and grilled mushrooms.

Second Breakfast:

A selection of sweet berries with fresh, whipped cream.

Elevenses:

Honeycakes and milk.

Luncheon:

Sizzling sausages and mash.

Afternoon Tea:

Seed-cake, buttered scones and jam with a fresh pot of tea.

Dinner:

Rabbit stew, with turnips, potatoes and carrots. Followed by a blackberry tart.

Supper:

A light mushroom soup with freshly baked warm rolls and butter.

Perfect manners

Hobbits are a very generous bunch and love to share. There's always a fresh pot of tea brewing, or some delicious cakes that have just been baked in a hobbit's house – perfect if a visitor comes calling and would like a little something to nibble on. They are also extremely polite, have very good manners and are the perfect hosts. This might sound like a good thing, and usually it is. However, sometimes hobbits can be a bit too generous and polite for their own good, as Bilbo found out to his cost. Not only did he end up with many more house guests than he expected, but he also ended up heading off across Middle-earth on an unexpected adventure!

BILBO BAGGINS

Most sensible hobbits seem to want a quiet life where nothing unexpected happens and no-one really notices them. However, sometimes Big Things happen and bring out the Tookish side of even the most sensible hobbit. More often than not the chosen hobbits don't even know that these Big Things will take them on an adventure that will change their lives forever!

While people might sing songs and tell tales of the great Kings of Gondor or the heroes of the Goblin Wars, some of the greatest heroes ever to have lived are actually hobbits from the Shire, and Bilbo Baggins is one of the greatest hobbit heroes ever.

The son of Bungo Baggins and Belladonna Took, Bilbo was born on September 22. Like most of the Baggins family, Bilbo and his parents lived near the town of Hobbiton. Bilbo spent his childhood growing up in Bag End, and after his parents died he became its owner.

Even from an early age there were some worrying signs that Bilbo had an 'odd' interest in adventure and excitement. As a young boy, whenever Gandalf came to visit, Bilbo would love to sit and listen to his exciting tales of dragons, Goblins, Giants and the rescuing of princesses. Most likely Gandalf could already see that this curious young hobbit was something special.

As Bilbo grew up he tried very hard to behave like a good Baggins. Bilbo had become a hobbit who didn't look particularly special or do anything unexpected or exciting. That was until he was 50 and Gandalf came to visit once more…

When Gandalf heard that Thorin Oakenshield was looking for a burglar to join his quest, he knew just the fellow to ask. Knowing that Bilbo's Tookish spirit was still alive and well, Gandalf convinced Bilbo to leave the Shire behind and join Thorin's adventure. Soon Bilbo found himself whisked away from his cosy hobbit-hole and off on a journey with 13 Dwarves across Middle-earth to steal treasure from a dragon!

The One Ring

Bilbo discovers many curious things on his adventures, but the plain gold ring he finds in the dark caves under the Misty Mountains turns out to be something extra special.

The Ring is actually an object of huge power. It is so powerful that only a true hero can manage the effort of carrying it and not be turned into something selfish and evil. When Bilbo finds the Ring he becomes one of the Ring-bearers and it changes his life forever.

GOLLUM

Bilbo meets Gollum in the caves under the Misty Mountains, where Gollum has lived in the dark for many years.

All that time alone in the darkness means that Gollum has become a hunched and twisted creature.

But Gollum didn't always look that way. In fact he was once a quite normal-looking creature called Sméagol. One day, long before Bilbo was born, Sméagol was out with his cousin when they found a plain gold ring. As it was his birthday, Sméagol wanted the Ring as his present. His cousin wanted to keep it for himself, though, and in a dreadful fight, Sméagol ended up killing his cousin and taking the Ring.

Like all the others after him who carry the Ring, Sméagol doesn't know that it is actually one of the most magical items in the world. The dark power of the Ring drives Sméagol half mad with greed, twisting his body and keeping him alive for over 500 years! For all that time he lives alone with his 'precious' Ring, scared that someone will come and take it away – which is just what happens when an ordinary hobbit stumbles across it one day.

FIRM FRIENDS

A sensible, practical hobbit like Bilbo can't really expect to have such grand adventures and triumph all on his own. Middle-earth can be a wild and dangerous place, and when you're fresh out of the Shire it's good to have some friendly faces to help you along the way.

Some companions, like Gandalf, were already legends in Middle-earth before Bilbo's adventures began. However, when he started out on his epic quest, most of his travelling companions were complete strangers, who were unknown in the world of hobbits. Here's a look at some of the heroes who made a name for themselves on their way to face a deadly dragon in the depths of the Lonely Mountain.

Thorin Oakenshield

Thorin was only a young prince when the fea... dragon Smaug attacked his home in Erebor, forc... him and his family out of their Kingdom and cla... all of their treasures. Without a home or riches, he was forced to wander Middle-earth until he eventually settled in the Blue Mountains, just to t... north-west of the Shire.

Here Thorin passed his days as a blacksmith an... waited for a time when he could once more claim his rightful place as the King under the Mountain.

The brave and fearless Thorin fought with great honour and skill in the Dwarven Wars. In the final battle Thorin's shield was shattered, so grabbing a wooden branch, he skilfully used it to defend himself. From that day on Thorin earned the name 'Oakenshield' and still enters battle with that oak branch strapped to his arm.

Many years later, Thorin gathers together a curious assortment of Dwarves to help him reclaim his family's kingdom. Almost ready to begin his quest to defeat Smaug and recover his family's fortune, Thorin needs just one more thing – a skilled burglar to help sneak into the dragon's lair and find the Arkenstone; the one piece of treasure that he values above all others.

Unfortunately for Bilbo, Gandalf thinks he's just the hobbit for the job, and recommends him to Thorin! At the beginning, Thorin doesn't trust Gandalf and thinks Bilbo would be more use cooking dinner than picking locks.

However, Gandalf convinces him and also provides an ancient map of the Lonely Mountain made by Thorin's grandfather, plus a mysterious key. Finally ready to begin his daring quest, Thorin and his Company set off for Erebor and the deadly fire-breathing dragon that lives below it.

During their quest, Thorin finds three very fine swords, which are covered in ancient runes. Thorin takes one of the swords for himself, and when Elrond translates the runes on it he finds out just how special it is. Forged long ago by the ancient Elves of Gondolin, it was used in the Goblin Wars. So great was the blade that it was named Orcrist by the Elves – and Biter by the Goblins!

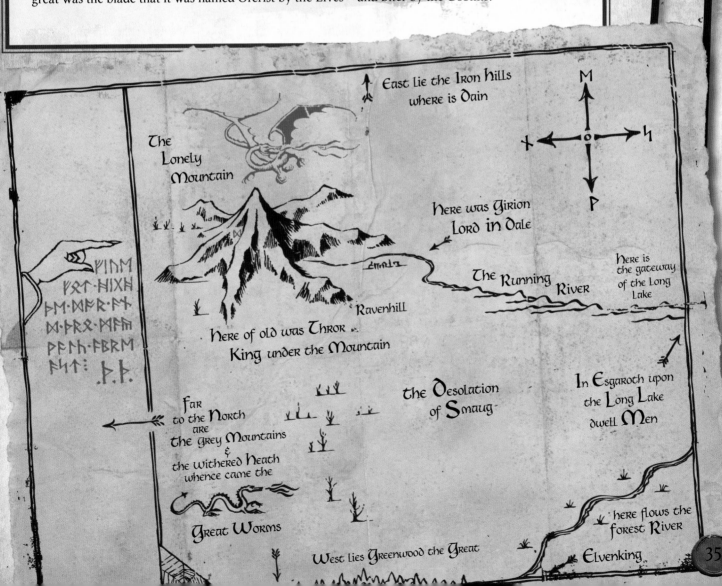

The Company of Dwarves

Along with Thorin, Bilbo is also accompanied on his quest to the Lonely Mountain by 12 other Dwarves. Some, like Bofur and his brother, Bombur, are more like hobbits than Dwarves and spend almost as much time as Bilbo wondering where the next meal is coming from! Bombur is actually the main cook for the Company and, if he had his way, would stop and make so many meals that even Bilbo would be full. Just like a hobbit, Bofur has a great love of music and delights in singing.

Bombur

Bifur

Bofur

Bifur is perhaps the strangest of Bilbo's travelling companio With a rusting Orc axe sticking out of his forehead, Bifur is enough to scare anyone off their dinner! He communicates v the occasional grunt or by waving his hands. Unlike many of other Dwarves in the group, Bifur is not from a noble family, but comes from a long line of miners and smiths.

Dwalin

Balin and his brother, Dwalin, are two of Thorin's closest friends and fiercest supporters. If Balin is wise and calm, Dwalin is more a Dwarf of action. One of the oldest members of the group, Balin is himself a Dwarf Lord and is always there with a gentle word of wisdom for his friends. As committed to the quest as his brother, Dwalin is a powerful fighter. Not the friendliest member of the group, he does not trust strangers easily – particularly if they happen to be Elves.

Balin

Kili

Fili

Not all of the Dwarves in the Company are as concerned with their bellies (though all of them certainly have healthy appetites). Fili and his brother Kili were both raised by their uncle, Thorin, and have joined the quest to help restore the ancient city of Erebor and write themselves into the history books. Both are skilled fighters who have led a quiet life so far (in Dwarf terms!) and are itching for their first taste of adventure.

Nori

Dori, Nori and Ori are brothers. Nori has spent a lot of his life using his skills to get into trouble and then using his wits to try and get out of it again. In fact, Nori joined the quest in the first place to get away from a spot of bother. Unfortunately the quest to the Lonely Mountain seems to have got him into more trouble than he left behind!

Dori

Ori

Unlike his brothers, Ori is quiet and prefers to spend his time drawing and writing in his journal, much like Bilbo. Often bossed about by the other members of the group, there are still times when he can surprise people with his determination and courage in the face of danger.

Dori is the strongest in the group and spends a lot of time looking out for his two brothers. He is usually one to expect the worst in every situation, particularly if Nori has had anything to do with things!

When you think of a Dwarf, chances are you will think of someone very much like Gloin. With a beard almost as large and wild as his temper, Gloin is not one to keep his opinions to himself. More likely to act than to think, he is one of the strongest and bravest of Thorin's companions.

Oin

Gloin

Gloin's brother, Oin, is the group's healer and is a genius with potions and medicine. Not directly related to Thorin, Oin and Gloin are actually Northern Dwarves, but have joined the quest through their sense of loyalty to Dwarves in general. Oin also has another reason for wanting the quest to succeed – he has spent quite a lot of his own money to pay for it!

Gandalf

Well before the great events on the way to the Lonely Mountain, Gandalf the Grey was already known as one of the most powerful Wizards in the world. One of the ancient protectors of Middle-earth, Gandalf is part of the White Council and has dedicated his life to guarding the world from evil.

Known as Mithrandir to the Elves, Gandalf not only helps Bilbo and his friends with their quest, but also ends up on his own adventure. When news reaches him that a bigger and more ancient evil has returned, he has to leave Bilbo and travel to the darkest corners of the world to try and uncover the truth.

While Gandalf is undoubtedly an amazing Wizard, there is more to him than great magical powers. Just like the hobbits for whom he has such affection, Gandalf is a person of many layers, with a quiet sense of humour and a love of the simple things in life. Perhaps that is why he enjoys his visits to the Shire so much and delights in using his powers to create magical shows to entertain the hobbits.

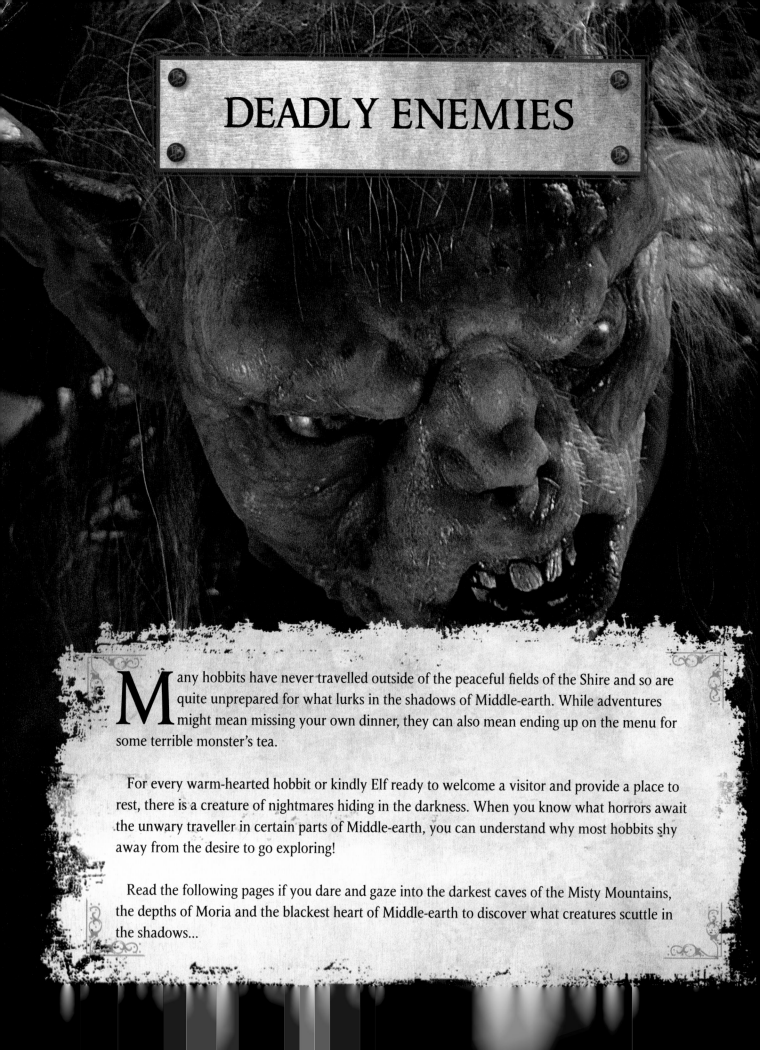

DEADLY ENEMIES

Many hobbits have never travelled outside of the peaceful fields of the Shire and so are quite unprepared for what lurks in the shadows of Middle-earth. While adventures might mean missing your own dinner, they can also mean ending up on the menu for some terrible monster's tea.

For every warm-hearted hobbit or kindly Elf ready to welcome a visitor and provide a place to rest, there is a creature of nightmares hiding in the darkness. When you know what horrors await the unwary traveller in certain parts of Middle-earth, you can understand why most hobbits shy away from the desire to go exploring!

Read the following pages if you dare and gaze into the darkest caves of the Misty Mountains, the depths of Moria and the blackest heart of Middle-earth to discover what creatures scuttle in the shadows...

Goblins

Goblins are about the size of a hobbit. If you're lucky enough to glimpse one and escape without being eaten, then you'll see that they are quite hunched, with large eyes, slimy skin and pointed ears. You're also more likely to smell them coming before you see them, as they live their lives in filth and darkness.

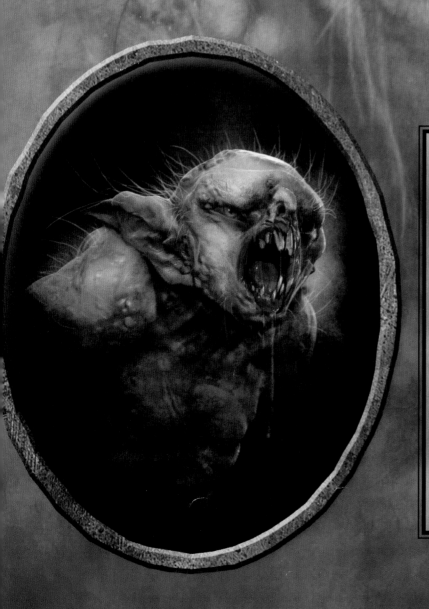

No one is quite sure where or when Goblins first appeared in Middle-earth, but they have always been vicious, cunning and evil. Goblins are fearsome warriors who rarely take prisoners – they are more likely to chop you into pieces for their next meal than keep you alive for questioning.

Most Goblins live in dark caves far below the Misty Mountains. One of their biggest cities is Goblin Town, near the High Pass above Rivendell. Hidden away in the shadows behind secret doors, the city spreads for mile after mile under the mountains. A maze of tunnels and caves, it is impossible to find your way through Goblin Town unless you know where you're going.

Goblin Town is the home of the Goblin King. Quite the largest Goblin you're ever likely to see (or smell), he is the absolute ruler of the Goblins. Over the years, the Goblins have fought many wars with the Dwarves and the Elves, who created special weapons that glow when Goblins are nearby.

   Because they live in underground caves, Goblins are very good at seeing in the dark as well as moving quickly through small tunnels. They are also extremely good at climbing. While they are as skilled as Dwarves at tunnelling and mining, they are nowhere near as expert at making weapons. Goblins prefer to take their equipment from their victims and are often armed with all sorts of rusty, dented and ancient weapons. Not that this makes them any less deadly, of course.

Orcs

As evil and foul as their Goblin relatives, Orcs have been a curse on Middle-earth for thousands of years. Larger than Goblins, they are about the same size as a Man, but more muscular. They live for a very long time and are incredibly tough and strong, making them deadly enemies and ideal soldiers for the forces of evil.

Ugly and dirty, Orcs are not the cleverest creatures. That doesn't mean they are stupid, however – they certainly have a keen sense for battle. Orcs can be found in many places through Middle-earth. If you are crazy enough to go looking for them, you might not live to tell the tale...

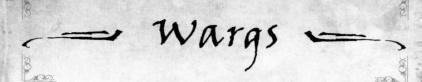

Wargs

Orcs are fearsome enough foes on their own, but they are ten times worse when they are riding their monstrous Wargs. Bred for battle, they are enormous and powerful creatures that would strike fear into even the bravest heart.

Wargs are like giant wolves – taller by far than any hobbit and twice as long as most horses! Covered in short, thick fur and with huge mouths full of razor sharp teeth, these horrible monsters are incredibly strong and fast. They are able to run for long distances without tiring and still have the strength to tear you apart at the end!

Wargs and their Orc riders often hunt in packs and there's not much that can stand in their way. While they have strong legs for running, they don't seem to be too good at climbing trees – something which is worth remembering if you ever encounter them!

Trolls

Enormous, mean and none too clever, Trolls are always on the lookout for something new to fill their bellies. They're not fussy about what they eat, though, and will happily feast on whatever it is they can catch – whether it's mutton, Man, Dwarf or hobbit!

While Trolls may be very strong and hard to fight, they do have one weakness – daylight. Like Goblins, they live mostly in dark caves and only come out at night. However, Trolls don't just stay away from sunlight because it hurts their eyes – it can also turn them to stone!

Goblins, Trolls, Wargs and Orcs aren't the only foul creatures waiting to pounce on Bilbo and his party. The dark places of Middle-earth are also full of giant spiders, unfriendly Wood Elves and their king, as well as all manner of other terrifying beasts. There's also one other creature that they need to keep in mind – the large fire-breathing dragon that waits at the end of their quest.

THE HOBBIT
AN UNEXPECTED JOURNEY
The World of Hobbits

Enter the amazing World of Hobbits.
Packed with photos from the new blockbuster movie,
this book will tell you all you need to know about these
amazing creatures – their appearance (short),
appetites (large), homes, friends, deadly foes
and much more.

ISBN 978-0-547-89873-5

9780547898735   50995

www.hmhbooks.com

$9.95 Ages 8 and up

Film / Fantasy
1112 / 1509946

NEW LINE CINEMA   MGM

T4-AZJ-090

Anna Jarvis

and the
Story of Mother's Day

coloring/activity book